C

Cooking

The Jesse Ashworth Cookbook

Stephen E. Stanley

Illustrations by the Author

Stonefield Publishing, 2011
Portland, Maine

Dearest Carol —

What a special and wonderful
week we have had.
Memories that will last
forever.
I am so lucky to be a
member of your special
family.
Thank you for all you have
done and love for me. —
I consider you my
sister —
Orchestrated with all
my love — always —

Pat

Revised Edition
2012

Preface

Like my fictional character Jesse Ashworth in the Jesse Ashworth mysteries, I began collecting recipes and cookbooks back in college. My family was full of good cooks, and I grew up taking home cooking for granted. It wasn't until I was older and started eating at other people's houses that I discovered that not everyone was good in the kitchen. When I had my first apartment in college it was a challenge to cook for myself. Fortunately I grew up watching my grandmother and mother in the kitchen, and though I had no skill at cooking, I also had no fear. They had made it look easy, but I found out it wasn't.

The first recipes I collected came from a supper at Portland's First Parish Church back in the early seventies. I remember painstakingly making Swedish meatballs by following a recipe I got from the cooking column of the *Portland Press Herald*. We parishioners all came with a covered dish and a recipe card. The cards were collected and taken to the copy machine, and I left with my first collection of Maine recipes.

As I traveled around the state, I stopped often at used bookstores, where I found a wealth of old Maine church and social organization cookbooks. People who like to cook, I found, were always willing to share their recipes and I began to collect recipes from different sources. The shepherd's pie recipe, for instance, I got from an Irish pub in Boston. Stifado and Moussaka recipes were inspired by the two summers I spent backpacking in Greece. And of course many recipes came from my mother and grandmother. In each case I've adapted the recipes to modern tastes and ingredients available in local supermarkets.

When *A Midcoast Murder* was first published, the main character, Jesse Ashworth, cooked as a sort of hobby. I had no idea that cooking would be one of the more popular aspects of the book. I began to get requests from readers for Jesse's recipes, so in the second edition I included the recipes at the end.

This is my version of white trash cooking. Simple, fresh ingredients simply prepared.

Stephen E. Stanley
June 2011

ISBN-13: 978-1463551483

ISBN-10: 1463551487

Printed in the United States of America.

Stonefield Publishing
Portland, Maine.

Second Edition 2012

Recipes from Jesse's Recipe Box.

In college in the 1970's, Jesse began to collect old church and community cookbooks from Maine. Restricted by a limited student budget, Jesse sought out recipes that were thrifty as well as flavorful. Many of the old recipes came from a time when great food variety was limited. Maine cooks were creative and managed to feed their families with few ingredients and fewer financial resources. Jesse has adapted many of these recipes, some which go back to colonial days, to reflect today's higher health consciousness.

Jesse has a few rules about ingredients. In baking, always use real butter and real vanilla extract, never margarine or imitation vanilla. Use meat and chicken sparingly, and when you do use it, try to obtain farm-raised organic meat, or free range poultry. The higher cost will be offset by the better flavor, and you will be supporting the small family farms, and not supporting the inhumane factory-farming agribusinesses.

Stephen E. Stanley

Main Dishes

Shepherd's Pie

This one-dish meal originates from England, where Shepherd's Pie refers to a dish made with lamb, and the American beef version is called Cottage Pie. Jesse was first introduced to the dish in the school lunch program, which inexplicitly called it Chinese Pie.

    1 lb. of ground beef
    1 cup of cooked, diced carrots.
    1 cup of cooked peas
    1 small onion
    1 can of creamed corn
    1 small can of whole corn
    1 cup of vegetable or beef broth
    3 tablespoons of flour
    salt and pepper

Brown one pound of ground beef with one chopped onion. Season with salt and pepper. Once brown add the carrots and peas. Add one cup of broth and flour and bring the meat mixture to a boil. Place the meat mixture in the bottom of a casserole dish. Place the creamed corn in a layer over the meat mixture and add the whole corn on top. Top the dish with mashed potatoes and place in a 350 degree oven for 35 minutes, or until the top of the potatoes begin to brown.

Confetti Bean Casserole
Slow Cooker

> Sweet Italian sausage ground or cut up
> 1 onion chopped
> 1 green pepper cut in slices
> 1 small can tomato sauce
> 1 can black beans
> 1 can white beans
> 1 small can chick peas
> 1 can red kidney beans
> 1 package frozen lima beans
> 1 small can yellow corn

Sauté sausage and onion place everything in slow cooker. Cook on low or simmer for six hours

Cola Meatloaf
Cola gives this meatloaf a sweet flavor

> 1 tablespoon mustard
> 1 tablespoon ketchup
> 1 chopped onion
> 1 cup bread crumbs
> 1 cup cola
> 1 lb ground beef
> 1 egg

Add more cola or breadcrumbs until you get the right consistency Place in a loaf pan and bake at 350 degrees for 45-60 minutes.

Beef Burgundy Casserole (oven version)

An easy and flavorful beef dish to serve over egg noodles.

Preheat oven to 300 degree

> 1 lb. lean chuck cut into cubes
> ½ cup red wine
> 1 can beef consommé
> salt and pepper
> 1 chopped onion
> ¼ cup bread crumbs
> ¼ cup flour
> 3 carrots, sliced thick

Mix all together, cover and bake for three hours

Chicken in White Wine and Yogurt.

> 4 chicken breast
> 4 tablespoon margarine
> 3 tablespoon flour
> ½ cup chicken stock
> ¾ cup plain low-fat yogurt
> ¼ cup white wine
> ½ cup sliced mushrooms

Bake chicken breast with margarine for 30 minutes at 350 degrees. In saucepan melt 2 tablespoon margarine, add flour and cook briefly. Add yogurt and wine until blended. Cover cooked breast with wine-yogurt mixture and add mushrooms. Bake uncovered for thirty minutes.

Bubble and Squeak

This is an English recipe that uses leftovers to create a hearty meal. There are a great many variations, but the most common elements are potato and cabbage. Here is Jesse's version. Depending on your leftovers, this will be a different dish every time.

> 1 cup of beef, pork, ham, of chicken, cut up into cubes.
> 1 cup of diced cooked potatoes
> 1 cup of shredded cabbage
> Leftover peas, carrots, or corn
> Any other leftovers you wish to add

Place ingredients into a well-greased fry pan. Fry until the potatoes begin to brown up.

Vegetable Pie

This is a tasty main dish for non meat eaters. A great way to use leftover vegetables.

1 cup cut-up, cooked asparagus (Other vegetables can be substituted.)
1 small onion diced
½ cup mushrooms
1 cup shredded cheddar cheese
1 ½ cups milk
¾ cup biscuit mix
3 eggs
1 teaspoon salt

Fry onions and mushrooms. Mix all ingredients together, place in a greased pie plate and bake at 400 degrees for 35 minutes.

Stuffed Hot Dogs

My grandparents raised four kids during the depression and the food rationing of WWII. My grandmother knew how to stretch her food dollars. Here is one of her recipes.

8 pieces of bacon
8 hot dogs
¼ cup vegetable oil
3 cups dried bread crumbs
1 teaspoon salt
¼ teaspoon pepper
1 teaspoon dried sage
½ cup water of vegetable stock
1 teaspoon celery seed

Cook onion and celery seed in oil. Add salt pepper and sage with bread crumbs and add water. Spilt hot dogs and stuff with dressing. Wrap each hot dog in bacon and secure with tooth picks. Place in pan and bake at 425 degrees for thirty minutes.

Stuffed Peppers (slow cooker)

An easy recipe for a cold day.

4 green bell peppers, seeded
1 lb. ground beef
1/3 cup bread crumbs
1 small diced onion
1 small can corn
1 can condensed tomato soup
1 tablespoon mustard

Mix beef, onion, bread crumbs, and corn. Stuff peppers with the mixture. Place in slow cooker. Mix tomato soup and mustard and pour over peppers. Cook on low for six hours.

American Chop Suey.

American Chop Suey is a dish created during the depression that continued to be a favorite during World War II when rationing was in effect. By the 1950's, is simplicity and cost made it one of America's most popular comfort foods. The recipe has many variations, but the basic ingredients are ground beef, elbow macaroni, and some type of tomato sauce. During war rationing, it was often made with sliced up hot dogs and tomato soup, as these sometimes were more readily available than ground beef and tomato sauce. Here is Jesse's version:

> 1 lb of ground beef
> 1 green pepper
> 1 onion
> 1 teaspoon red pepper flakes
> 1 box elbow macaroni
> 1 teaspoon Italian seasoning
> 1 package of mushrooms
> 1 can diced tomatoes
> 1 can tomato sauce
> ¼ cup red wine
> 1 cup shredded cheese

Chop up onion, green pepper, and mushrooms with red pepper flakes. Add ground beef and brown. Drain off grease and add tomato sauce, wine, and diced tomato. Simmer on low for 10 minutes. Boil macaroni according to directions. Drain macaroni and add sauce, top with cheese. Tofu can be used in place of beef to make a vegetarian version.

Chicken in the Pan

This is a great recipe for an electric fry pan. It was originally a one-pot meal from colonial times. My mother often made it for company.

4 boneless, skinless chicken breasts.
4 onions cut up
4 medium potatoes cut up
8 carrots, peeled and sliced
A handful of green beans, cut up (for color)
1 ½ cups chicken or vegetable stock.

Brown chicken in oil at 350 degrees. When brown add vegetables with the stock. Reduce heat to 250 and simmer until chicken and vegetables are done.

Baked Beans (slow cooker)

Beans are a traditional New England dinner for Saturday nights. Leftover beans are then served for breakfast.

2 cups of dry beans, cover with water soak over night. Drain and place in oiled crock pot. Add:

1 teaspoon salt
2 tablespoons molasses
2 teaspoon dry mustard
1 medium onion cut up
2 tablespoons ketchup
1 tablespoons Worcestershire sauce
¼ cup olive oil
3 cups vegetable stock

Cover beans with vegetable stock and cook on low for 6-8 hours. Add stock or water as needed.

Chicken Cordon Bleu (Slow Cooker)

Boneless chicken breasts; one per person.
¼ lb sliced cheese
¼ lb sliced ham
1 can condensed cream of chicken or cream of mushroom soup

Place breasts in plastic wrap and pound flat. Layer thin ham slices and thin slices of cheese on top of breasts. Roll each breast and secure with a tooth pick.
Place in oiled slow cooker . Cover with soup. Cool on low.

Sweet and Sour Kielbasa

Kielbasa
¼ cup catsup
½ cup beer
3 tablespoon brown sugar
1 tablespoon vinegar
2 tablespoons brown mustard.

Cut kielbasa into ½ inch slices and simmer in sauce for 30 minutes.

Oven Beef Stew

2 tablespoons flour
2 teaspoon salt
Pepper to taste
2 cups water
1 lb stew beef
1 cup condensed tomato soup
1 chopped onion
3 potatoes
2 chopped carrots
2 tablespoons celery seed

Combine salt , pepper and flour and dredge meat. Brown meat in butter. Place in oven proof dish the meat, soup , onion, and 1 cup of water at 375 for one hour. Add vegetables and the rest of the water and cook for another hour.

Tim's Grilled Burgers
Tim does the outside cooking.

1 lb ground beef
¼ cup cracker crumbs
1 tablespoon yellow mustard
1 tablespoon Worcestershire sauce
1 egg
Salt, pepper

Mix and divide into 4 burgers. Cook on a preheated grill.

Spaghetti Pie

I first had this at a church supper. Hearty and good-tasting, this recipe is even better warmed over.

1 8 oz package of spaghetti (broken into little pieces.)
2 tablespoons olive oil
1 large jar of spaghetti sauce
1/3 cup grated parmesan cheese
1 egg
1 ½ lb ground beef (or half beef and half ground Italian sausage)
1 onion
½ teaspoon oregano
1 cup cottage or ricotta cheese
1 package mixed shredded cheese.
¼ cup red wine

Cook spaghetti, drain and place in bowl. Add egg and parmesan cheese. Spread mixture evenly in 9" x 13" pan. Brown meat and onion, stir in spaghetti sauce, red wine, sugar, and oregano with the meat.

Spread cottage or ricotta cheese. Sprinkle half of the shredded cheese over cheese mixture. Cover with meat mixture. Sprinkle remaining shredded cheese and bake at 350 for 30 minutes.

Cheeseburger Pie
Another church supper recipe.

One lb. ground beef
1 chopped onion
½ teaspoon. salt
½ teaspoon pepper
1 cup cheddar cheese
1   cup Milk
1/2 cup biscuit mix
2 eggs
¼ cup grated parmesan cheese

Brown meat with onions and peppers. Drain. Mix biscuit mixture, salt, pepper, eggs, parmesan cheeses, and milk. Grease a 9" pie pan. Spread meat in pan. Sprinkle cheese over meat. Pour batter over cheese. Bake at 400 degrees for 30 minutes.

Lentil Loaf
2 cups cooked lentils
1 cup cooked brown rice
1 tablespoon Worcestershire sauce
1 small onion chopped
1 egg
¼ cup grated carrot
1 cup bread crumbs
¼ cup chopped walnuts
¼ cup vegetable stock
1 tablespoon catsup
2 teaspoon thyme or oregano
Mix together and form a loaf. Bake at 350 degrees for one hour.

Slow Cooker Lasagna
Easy make ahead meal

> 1 lb ground beef or Italian sausage
> 1 chopped onion
> 1 (28 oz) can tomato sauce
> 1 (6oz) can tomato paste
> 1 ½ teaspoon salt
> 1 teaspoon dried Italian seasoning
> 12 oz cottage cheese
> ¼ cup grated parmesan or Romano cheese
> ½ cup shredded cheddar cheese
> 12 (oz) uncooked lasagna noodles

Brown beef and onion in fry pan, drain excess grease. Add tomato sauce and tomato paste, salt and spices. Spoon some meat sauce of the bottom of the slow cooker. Add a layer of uncooked noodles (break to fit the pot is needed.) Top with cheese mixture. Add another layer of meat sauce. Layer more noodles, cheese and meat sauce until used up. Cook on low for about five hours.

Mac and cheese
Better than the box version and just as easy

> 1 box of macaroni cooked *al dente*
> 1 onion minced
> 3 eggs
> 1 can evaporated milk
> 1 cup cheddar cheese
> 1 cup Monterey jack cheese
> ½ cup grated parmesan cheese
> ½ lb sliced deli ham cup up

Sauté onion, mix all ingredients. Bake in greased casserole dish at 375 for 35 minutes.

Crustless Spinach Quiche

3 eggs
1 chopped onion
1 cup milk
1 cup flour
1 teaspoon salt
1 teaspoon baking powder
1 package frozen spinach drained
16 oz shredded cheese

Butter pie pan. Mix all ingredients. Bake at 400 degrees for 25-30 minutes.

Beef Stroganoff (Slow Cooker)

3 lbs beef cubed into one inch cube.
One can beef consume
1 small can tomato paste
1 package sliced mushrooms
1 small onion, chopped.
1 package cream cheese

Sauté onions and mushrooms. Put all ingredients except cream cheese in slow cooker for 6 to 8 hours on low. Add cream cheese one half hour before serving. Serve over noodles, rice, or potatoes.

Moussaka

A Greek casserole recipe brought back from my travels

1 ½ lb ground beef or lamb
3 medium eggplants
½ cup olive oil
salt and pepper
2 onions
1 clove garlic
2 tomatoes chopped
1 can tomato puree
½ teaspoon allspice
1 teaspoon parsley

Topping

3 tablespoons butter
3 tablespoons flour
3 cups of milk
3 eggs
½ cup grated parmesan cheese

Peel and slice eggplant, brush with oil and bake at 350 degrees for 15 minutes or until tender
Sauté onion and garlic, add meat and brown. Add tomatoes puree, herbs and spiced. Stir well and simmer for 15 minutes.
Grease baking dish, arrange meat mixture and eggplant slices in layers.
Topping:
In a saucepan melt butter, flour, milk and bring to a boil. Take on heat and allow to cool. Add eggs and cheese and pour over meat and eggplant. Bake at 350 degrees for one hour.

Baked Scallops

>1 lb scallops
>4 tablespoons butter
>10-20 crackers crumbled
>Salt and pepper

Melt butter in a shallow glass baking dish. Wash and dry scallops. Put cracker crumbs in a pie plate. Roll scallops in melted butter, then roll in cracker crumbs and place bake in baking dish. Make sure the scallops are not touching. Bake at 400 degrees for 20 minutes. Serves two.

Church Supper Chicken Casserole

>1 cup elbow macaroni
>1 can condensed cream of chicken soup
>1 small can of mushrooms
>1 ½ cup cut up chicken
>1 cup mayonnaise
>1 green pepper sliced
>1 medium onion diced
>1 tablespoon celery seed
>2 cups shredded sharp cheddar cheese
>½ cup bread crumbs or cracker crumbles

Cook macaroni and drain. Add other ingredients and pour into greased casserole dish. Top with bread crumbs. Bake at 350 degree for 35 minutes.

Beef Burgundy (Stove Top Version)

> 2 lbs stew beef cut into one inch cubes
> Flour for dredging
> 1 green pepper
> Salt and pepper
> 1 teaspoon paprika
> 3 large onions, sliced
> 2 carrots shredded
> 1 teaspoon celery seed
> 1 tablespoon catsup
> 2 cups red wine

Dredge meat in flour, salt, paprika and pepper. Brown meat in oil. Add the rest of the ingredients. Simmer for two to three hours until tender. Serve over buttered noodles.

Fish Cakes
A traditional meal includes baked beans.

> 1 lb flakey white fish, such as cod, haddock, or
hake
> 4 medium size potatoes
> ¼ teaspoon pepper
> 1 egg

Poach fish in water with ½ cup white wine or 1 tablespoon lemon until flaky or about five minutes. Boil potatoes. Drain fish and potatoes and place in a mixing bowl with egg and pepper. Mix together and form into patties and fry until golden brown.

Souvlaki

1 pound pork loin
1 lemon
2 tablespoons olive oil
½ cup water
Salt and pepper

Cut pork into one inch cubes. Make a marinade with the juice of the lemon, water, and olive oil. Let the meat marinate for at least one hour. Arrange meat on a stick or spear and cook over an open flame or barbecue grill.

Swedish Meatballs

1 small onion
¼ cup bread crumbs
1 ½ lb of ground beef
1 egg
Salt and pepper
1 tablespoon worcestershire sauce

Sauce:

1 can beef stock
½ cup sour cream
2 tablespoons butter
2 tablespoons flour
3 tablespoons seedless raspberry jam

Finely chop onion and sauté until translucent. Add onions to beef, egg, bread crumbs, salt, and pepper. Add milk if mixture is too stiff. Roll into balls. Place meatballs on a rack . Place the rack on a cookie sheet which has been lines with aluminum foil. Bake at 375 for 30 minutes.

Place sauce ingredients in a sauce pan over medium heat. Wisk sauce until thick.

Place meatballs in a baking dish or casserole dish. Pour sauce over meatballs and serve.

Pork Chops and Apples

    1 teaspoon sage
    6 center cut pork chops
    1 lb. sliced carrots
    1 cup sliced onions
    1 lb peeled and sliced apples
    ¼ cup brown sugar

Grease 9 x 12 pan. Layer ingredients and cover with foil. Bake for 2 hours at 350.

Canadian Chicken Pot Pie

    1 pound skinless, boneless cooked chicken breast
halves – cubed
    6 cooked link sausages cut into small pieces
    1 cup sliced carrots
    1 cup frozen green peas
    1/3 cup butter
    1 small chopped onion
    1/3 cup all-purpose flour
    1/2 teaspoon salt
    1/4 teaspoon celery seed
    1 3/4 cups chicken broth
    2/3 cup milk
    2   unbaked pie crusts

Preheat oven to 425 degrees. In a saucepan, combine carrots, and peas. Add water to cover and boil for 15 minutes. Remove from heat, drain and set aside. Add cooked chicken and sausage.

In another saucepan over medium heat, cook onions in butter until soft and translucent. Stir in flour, salt, pepper, and celery seed. Slowly stir in chicken broth and milk. Simmer over medium-low heat until thick. Remove from heat and set aside.

Cover pie plate with one pie crust and place the chicken and vegetable mixture in bottom. Pour hot liquid mixture over the meat. Cover with top crust. Make several small slits in the top.

Bake in the preheated oven for 30 to 35 minutes, or until pastry is golden brown and filling is bubbly. Cool for 10 minutes before serving.

New England Boiled Dinner

 3 pounds corned beef
2 medium turnips peeled and cut up
6 large carrots
6 potatoes peeled and quartered
1 medium head of cabbage
1 bay leaf
6 pepper corns
3 whole cloves
6 whole beets

Cover corned beef with water, add bay leaf, pepper corns, and cloves. Bring to a boil. Cut heat back to a simmer and cook for three hours or until the meat is tender. Remove meat and let cool. Remove pepper corn and cloves.

Add potatoes, carrots, turnips, and cabbage to the water and cook until tender. Cook beets in a separate pan.

Arrange sliced corn beef and vegetables on a platter and serve.

The Maine version often substitutes smoked shoulder for corn beef.

The Canadian version adds split yellow peas, cooked in a mesh bag.

Leftovers can be cup up and fried to make corned beef hash. With beets added it become red flannel hash.

Haddock Bake

1 lb haddock fillets
¼ cup lemon juice
½ cup mayonnaise
½ cup parmesan cheese
1 teaspoon prepared mustard
1 teaspoon paprika

Line 9 x 13 in pan with foil' Place fillets in pan and sprinkle with lemon juice. Combine mayo and mustard and spread over fish. Sprinkle cheese over fish and finish with paprika. Bake for 30 minutes at 400 degrees.

Baked Fish and Shrimp

2 lbs haddock fillet
¼ cup grated onion
2 tablespoons butter
1 beaten egg
½ cup cracker crumbs
1 can cream of shrimp soup
1 lb cooked shrimp

Place fillets in greased baking dish. Place shrimp on top. Combine the rest of the ingredients and pour over fish. Bake one hour at 375 degrees.

Soups, Stews, & Chowders

Maine Clam Chowder

    1 quart fresh clams or 2 cans whole clams
    3 slices of bacon
    1 small onion
    4 small potatoes diced
    Salt and pepper to taste
    1 quart of milk
    2 cans evaporated milk
    2 tablespoons butter

Fry bacon in the bottom of a large cooking kettle. Remove bacon and add onions and cook, careful not to burn. Add diced potatoes and cover with just enough water to barely cover the potatoes and cook until potatoes are soft. Chop up fresh clams and cook for three minutes. If using canned clams omit cooking. Add fresh and canned milk and butter. Let sit in the refrigerator at least two hours and preferably over night. Reheat slowly over low heat and do not let it boil.

Lobster Stew

Fresh lobster makes the best stew. Save the juice when you crack open the shells and add to the stew.

2 cups cooked lobster meat
1 small onion
½ stick butter
2 cups light cream
2 cups of milk

Melt butter in large saucepan with onion. Add lobster meat and juice and cook for three minutes. Add milk and cream and refrigerate overnight. Reheat slowly.

Chicken Soup

1 broiler chicken
1 quart water
1 large diced onion
1 tablespoon celery seed
5 carrots sliced
3 large potatoes
3 chicken bouillon cubes
3 tablespoons flour.

Place chicken in water with onion and celery seed. Add bouillon cubes. Simmer until chicken falls off the bone. Remove chicken and let cool. Skim any foam off the water. Simmer carrots and potatoes until tender. Remove chicken meat from the bones and add to soup. Remove one cup of broth and add flour to thicken, then add back to soup. Serve with fresh biscuits.

Squash Soup

This recipe came from a Vermont restaurant

2 large squashes cup up and microwaved.
2 cup chicken or vegetable broth
2 tablespoon butter
1 package cream cheese.
4 tablespoon honey
1 tablespoon salt
¼ teaspoon nutmeg
¼ teaspoon ginger
¼ cup milk.

Heat slowly and put in blender, or use an emersion blender to create a smooth soup.

Stifado (Greek Stew)

I spent two summers backpacking through Greece and returned home with a love of Greek food. The aroma of this cooking will bring neighbors to your door.

> 3 lbs stew beef
> 1 tablespoon brown sugar
> ½ cup butter
> 1 bay leaf
> 2 pounds peeled onions
> 1/8 teaspoon ground cloves
> 1 (6 oz.) can tomato paste
> 1/8 teaspoon cinnamon
> ½ cup red wine
> ¼ teaspoon cumin
> 2 tablespoon wine vinegar
> 2 tablespoon raisins

Cut beef into one-inch cubes. Season with salt and pepper. Melt butter in Dutch oven. Add meat and onions. Mix tomato paste, wine vinegar, and brown sugar and pour over meat and onion. Add bay leaf, spices, and raisins to pot. Cover and simmer for 3 hours.

Crab and Corn Chowder.

Jesse always makes this in October to celebrate autumn.

1 lb fresh cooked crabmeat.
2 medium potatoes diced
½ cup chopped onion
3 ears of corn
1 small can of creamed corn
4 tablespoons butter
1 cup half and half
1 cup milk
Salt and pepper
1 can condensed milk

Boil onion and potatoes until tender. In pot melt butter and sauté crabmeat for 2 minutes. Steam corn and cut off of the cob. Add potato, onion, and corn. Stir in milk and half and half. Add creamed corn. Take off stove and place overnight in refrigerator. Heat to serve.

Vegetarian Slow Cooker Chile
A very hearty vegetarian dish served at a church supper

½ cup olive oil

2 teaspoon salt

4 onions chopped   ½ teaspoon black pepper

1 green pepper sliced

1 red pepper sliced

6 tablespoon chili powder

2 teaspoon cumin

2 tablespoon oregano

1 (14 oz) Package of firm tofu, drained and finely cubed

2 cans drained black beans

2 cans drained red beans

2 tablespoon vinegar

1 tablespoon hot sauce

2 cans crushed tomatoes

¼ cup ground carrots

Brown peppers and onion with the tofu in oil until slightly browned. Pour all ingredients in slow cooker and cook on low for 6 to 8 hours.

Beef and Sweet Potato Stew

2 lbs of stew meat cut into one inch cubes
3 large sweet potatoes
¾ cup barley
2 small onions chopped
2 table spoons olive oil
2 cans chicken stock
½ teaspoon red pepper

Sauté onions in olive oil until
Cut up sweet potatoes into small chunks
Add all ingredients to crock pot and cook on low heat for six hours

Canadian Bean Soup
A great hearty soup for a cold day

1 pound sausage meat
1 medium onion
1 can great northern beans, rinsed and drained
1 can diced tomatoes
1 can chicken broth
1 teaspoon Italian seasoning
Salt and pepper

Brown the meat and onion in a fry pan. Place the ingredients into a crock pot and cook on low for six to eight hours.

Sides, Sauces, & Stuff

Home Made Mayo-type dressing

This is a very old recipe used for lobster salad and egg salad. It comes from a time before commercial mayo was readily available. It is a great addition to macaroni salads. Eggs are cooked to avoid potential food poisoning.

1 ½ tablespoon sugar
dash pepper
1 teaspoon salt
1 teaspoon dry mustard
1 tablespoon flour
1 beaten egg
¾ cups milk
¼ cup vinegar
2 tablespoon butter

Mix all ingredients together in the top of a double boiler. Set the mixture over boiling water. Stir until thick. Removes from heat. Add the butter and stir. Place in the refrigerator for at least two hours.

Ambrosia Fruit Salad

A cool fruit salad treat on a hot day.

1 can (11oz) can mandarin oranges -drained
1 can (20 oz) pineapple chunks –drained
1/3 cup shredded coconut
½ cup miniature marshmallows
½ plain yogurt

Mix together and chill. Add mint leaves or maraschino cherries to garnish.

Carrot Ring

A great visual side dish for a buffet.

>   1 lb carrots sliced and cooked
>   1 small onion
>   3 tablespoon milk
>   1 tablespoon butter
>   1 teaspoon salt
>   3 beaten eggs

Mash and mix all ingredients and place in oiled ring mold. Set mold in a pan of water and bake at 350 degrees for forty minutes. Unmold onto a plate and serve with cooked peas in the middle.

Bean Salad

1 can each drained kidney beans, chick peas, white beans, black beans
1 small can of corn
½ lb of cooked green beans
1 package frozen lima beans cooked
1 chopped onion
1/3 cup sugar
1/3 cup vinegar
1 teaspoon dry mustard
¼ cup oil.

Combine all ingredients and chill.

Roast Potatoes

Cut up potatoes and place in a plastic bag.
Add one chopped onion, salt and pepper
¼ cup bread crumbs to the bag.
Add 2 tablespoon olive oil and shake bag.
Bake at 350 until done, about 50 minutes.

New Potatoes and Peas

Peel and cook new potatoes in boiling water. Add 1 package frozen peas and cook until peas are ready. Drain, add ½ cup of heavy cream and 2 tablespoon butter, Salt and pepper and serve.

Minted Peas

Cook frozen peas in water. Drain, add butter and ¼ cup crème de menthe. Serve.

Red Cabbage

Cut red cabbage into wedges and steam for about 30 minutes. Toss cabbage with butter and olive oil. Add 2 tablespoon of horse radish and serve.

Copper Pennies

1 lb carrots, cut and cooked
1 onion chopped
1 bell pepper chopped
1/3 cup cooking oil
3/4 cup sugar
1/2 cup cider vinegar
1 tsp. prepared mustard
1 tsp. Worcestershire sauce
dash of black pepper

Place carrots, bell pepper, and onions in bowl. Mix all remaining ingredients and pour over vegetables. Refrigerate for at least 24 hours.

Vegetarian Stuffing

1 lb bread cubes
1 chopped onion
1 package sliced mushrooms
1 chopped red bell pepper
1 can vegetable stock
1 teaspoon celery seed
1 can condensed mushroom soup
2 eggs beaten
1 teaspoon thyme
1 teaspoon rosemary

Mix together and bake in 9x9 pan at 350 one hour.

Scallop Potatoes

> 6 medium potatoes sliced thin
> 1 medium onion minced
> ¼ cup butter
> 6 tablespoons flour
> ¼ cup grated parmesan cheese
> 1 can evaporated milk
> Salt and pepper

Boil potatoes in salted water for 15 minutes. Drain. In a casserole dish layer potatoes, place minced onion on top sprinkle with flour, cheese, salt and pepper. Add a tablespoon of butter. Repeat layering. Pour milk over potatoes and bake in oven at 375 for one hour.

Barbecue Sauce

> 1 chopped onion
> ¼ cup oil
> 1 cup water
> ½ cup catsup
> ½ cup molasses
> ¼ cup sugar
> 2 tablespoons vinegar
> 2 tablespoons Worcestershire sauce
> 1 beef bouillon cube

Fry onion in oil, add all other ingredients and simmer for 20 minutes.

Maine Dandelion Greens

Millions of Dollars are spent every year in an attempt to remove this plant from lawns. In Maine the dandelion is valued for its healthful properties. A native of Eurasia, it was most likely brought to North America by the early settlers. Its blossoms are used to make wine, its roots are roasted as a coffee substitute, and its dried leaves are used to make an herbal tea as a spring tonic. Its fresh leaves are good in a salad, but its most popular use is as cooked greens in early spring. Free for the picking!

Fresh dandelion greens
3 pieces of bacon

Dig greens in early spring before the blossoms appear. Wash thoroughly to remove any grit from the soil. Place in boiling water with three strips of bacon. Cook until tender. Serve buttered or with cider vinegar.

Horiatiki: **Greek Salad**

> 1 Cucumber
> 1 Green pepper
> 1 small onion
> 6 black olives
> 2 Tomatoes
> ¼ pound Feta cheese
> 3 tablespoons olive oil
> Salt and pepper
> Olive oil

Slice vegetables and arrange on plate. Pour olive oil over the salad and top with a feta cheese. Salt and pepper to taste.

Orange Beets

8 medium beets
1 cup orange juice
2 teaspoons corn starch
¼ cup honey
2 tablespoons butter

Cook beets in water until tender. Peel and slice, and keep warm in a covered pan.

In a saucepan combine orange juice, cornstarch, and honey, and beat with a fork until smooth. Bring to a boil and stir for two minutes. Add butter and stir until melted. Pour over beets.

Honey Roasted Vegetables

2 sweet potatoes, peeled and quartered
3 carrots, peeled and thickly sliced
½ cup walnuts
¼ cup honey

Preheat oven to 375, Toss all the ingredients together and place in baking dish. Bake for one hour.

Bread, Biscuits, & Muffins

Banana Muffins

Jesse often brings muffins to work. This is one of his favorites.

>   2 eggs
>   ½ cup molasses
>   2 cups of flour
>   2 teaspoon baking power
>   ¼ cup of oil
>   1 teaspoon vanilla
>   1 teaspoon salt
>   2 ripe bananas
>   1/8 cup sugar

Mix ingredients and bake at 400 degrees for 25 minutes.

Cornmeal Biscuits

These biscuits are especially good with soups, stews, and chowders. Preheat oven to 425 degrees

>   1 ½ cups unbleached flour
>   ½ cup cornmeal
>   1 tablespoon baking powder
>   ½ teaspoon salt
>   5 tablespoon butter
>   ¾ milk

Mix all dry ingredients and cut in the cold butter. Add milk and stir. Knead dough and cut into biscuits. Bake 12-15 minutes.

Easy Biscuits

Jesse uses this recipe on busy days.

2 cups flour
3 teaspoon baking powder
½ teaspoon salt
¾ cup sour cream
½ teaspoon baking soda
1 tablespoon cold water

Mix all ingredients. Add more water if needed. Form into a soft dough and shape or cut into biscuit. Bake at 450 degree for about 12 minutes.

Donut Muffins

2 cups flour
1 teaspoon soda
½ cup oil
½ teaspoon nutmeg
1 cup sugar
2 eggs
1 cup plain yogurt
1 tablespoon vanilla

Bake in greased muffin pan in a 350 degree oven for 20 minutes. Brush tops with melted butter and dust with sugar and cinnamon mix.

Applesauce Muffins

1 ½ cups applesauce
1/3 cup brown sugar
1 cup whole wheat flour
1/3 cup melted butter
1 egg
1 teaspoon soda
½ teaspoon salt
1 teaspoon baking powder
1 ½ cup white flour
½ teaspoon cinnamon

Mix all ingredients together and bake in a 350 degree oven for 20 minutes.

New England Corn Bread.

There are two versions of cornbread: Southern and New England. Southern cornbread doesn't use sugar and New England cornbread does.

1 cup flour
1 cup corn meal
4 tablespoons sugar
1 tablespoon baking powder
½ teaspoon salt
2 eggs
1 cup sour cream
¼ cup oil
1 tablespoon honey or molasses

Mix all ingredients together. Bake at 425 degrees: 25 minutes for a 9 x 9 greased pan. 15 minutes for muffins.

Blueberry Muffins

1 egg
1 ½ cup flour
½ cup plain yogurt
½ cup sugar
¼ cup oil
2 teaspoon baking powder
½ teaspoon salt
1 tablespoon vanilla
1 cup blue berries (other berries can be substituted)

Mix all ingredients together and bake in a greased muffin pan at 400 degrees for 20 minutes.

Egg Bread (for bread machine)
This make a 1 ½ lb loaf

2 eggs
1 cup warm water
2 tablespoon oil
2 tablespoon sugar
1 ½ teaspoon salt
2 cups white flour
1 cup whole wheat flour
1 ½ teaspoon yeast.

Use basic setting on machine.

Cranberry Scones

¼ cup shortening
¼ cup brown sugar
½ cup sugar
2 ½ cups flour
4 teaspoon baking soda
½ teaspoon salt

Cut above ingredients together. Then add:

1 cup milk
1 egg
1 tablespoon vanilla
1/2 cup cranberries

Mix dough until soft, roll out and cut into wedges. Bake at 425 degrees for 15 minutes. Brush with a glaze made with 2 tablespoons of apricot jam and 1 tablespoon of water.

Biscuits (Food Processor)

Preheat oven to 400
1 ¾ cup flour
½ teaspoon salt
3 teaspoon baking powder
½ teaspoon soda
6 tablespoon cold butter
2 tablespoon shortening

Place dry mixture in food processor and pulse until coarsely mixed.
Add ¾ milk and pulse until combined. Roll out, cut biscuits and bake on ungreased pan at 400 for 12 minutes.

Dumplings
Great on homemade soups

1 cup flour
2 teaspoons baking powder
½ teaspoon salt
1 egg
½ cup (scant) milk to moisten.

Mix and drop into simmering soup, using a table spoon for each dumpling. Cover and cook for 10 minutes.

Bakewell Cream Biscuits.

Almost every kitchen in Maine has a can of Bakewell Cream. This New England leavening agent in made right here in Maine. It makes lighter, fluffier biscuits than you can get anywhere. If it is not available in your store, you can order it on the internet.

2 cups flour
2 teaspoons Bakewell Cream
1 teaspoon baking soda
½ teaspoon salt
¼ cup cold butter
¾ cup milk

Preheat the oven to 475°F. Lightly grease a baking sheet, or line with parchment. Whisk the dry ingredients together in a bowl. Cut in the butter till the mixture is crumbly; some larger, pea-sized pieces of butter may remain intact. Add the milk, stirring till everything is moistened. Turn the dough out onto a clean work and roll out Cut the biscuits with a round cutter. Place them on the baking sheet. Brush their tops with melted butter. Bake for 5 minutes, then turn off the oven. Leave in the oven for an additional 5 to 10 minutes, till they're golden brown.

Sweet Endings

Quick Lemon Cheese Cake

Another time-saving dessert.

> 1 package of cream cheese
> 1 can lemon pie filling
> 1 graham cracker pie shell

Whip room-temperature cream cheese until fluffy, add lemon pie filling and whip until combined and fluffy. Put in pie shell and refrigerate. Serve with whipped cream.

Two-minute Key Lime Pie.

A tasty pie when you don't have the time or the inclination to make a multi-step dessert.

> 2 cans sweetened condensed milk
> ½ cup lime juice
> One graham cracker pie shell.

Mix sweetened condensed milk and lime juice together until it begins to thicken. Place in pie shell, chill and serve with whipped cream.

Sour Cream Chocolate Cake

Rhonda loves this cake! Jason and Monica requested it for their wedding cake.

    1 egg
    1 teaspoon soda
    ½ cup cocoa
    ½ teaspoon salt
    ½ cup oil
    1 tablespoon vanilla
    1 ½ cup flour
    ½ cup sour cream
    1 cup brown sugar
    ½ cup hot coffee

Mix all ingredients together. Pour into a greased and floured tube pan. Bake at 350 degree for 40-45 minutes. Finish with a dusting of powdered sugar.

Red Velvet Cake

There are many variations of the Urban Legend that go with this cake. Red Velvet Cake was a dessert created at the Waldorf-Astoria in New York City in the 1920's. According to the legend, a woman in 1930 asked for the recipe for the cake. She received the recipe and a bill for thirty dollars. Indignant, she spread the recipe in a chain letter. Beet juice can be used instead of red food coloring.

2 ½ cups of flour
1 ½ cups of sugar
2 teaspoon cocoa
1 teaspoon soda
1 teaspoon salt
2 eggs
1 tablespoon white vinegar
½ cup oil
1 cup plain yogurt
¼ cup red food coloring (or 2 oz. bottle)
1 tablespoon vanilla

Mix all ingredients together. Pour into three greased and floured 8-inch pans. Bake at 350 degrees for 30 minutes.

Frosting:
½ stick of butter
8 oz cream cheese
1 lb box powered sugar
1 teaspoon vanilla
Blend together and spread on cake.

Honey and Molasses Cake

This is a recipe from WWII when sugar was rationed.

1 ¼ cup of flour
¼ teaspoon cinnamon
1 teaspoon baking soda
¼ teaspoon cloves
¼ teaspoon salt
¼ teaspoon allspice
¼ teaspoon nutmeg
¼ cup honey
1 egg
½ molasses
¼ cup oil
½ cup boiling water

Preheat oven to 350. Mix all ingredients together, adding boiling water last. Bake in a tube pan for 35 minutes.

Molasses Pie

This is the Maine recipe similar to the southern version of Shoo fly pie.
Preheat oven to 400 Thaw one frozen pie crust, or make one pie crust from scratch.

Combine in Bowl:

> 1 cup of flour
> 5 tablespoon butter
> 2/3 cup of brown sugar
> Mash until crumbly

In a separate bowl:

> 1 cup of molasses
> 1 egg
> 1 teaspoon baking soda
> 1 cup boiling water

Take half of the crumb mixture and molasses mix and pour into piecrust. Top with the remaining crumb mixture. Bake for 10 minutes and reduce heat to 350 for 20-30 minutes. Serve with whipped cream

Blueberry Cream Cheese Pie

This is a great way to enjoy fresh Maine blueberries.

> 1 baked pie shell
> 1 tablespoon lemon juice
> 4 cups of fresh blueberries
> 1 (6oz) package of cream cheese
> ¾ cup water
> ½ powdered sugar
> ¼ cup of tapioca
> whipped cream

Simmer 2 cups of blueberries in water for 4 minutes. Add combined sugar and tapioca to the cooking fruit. Continue until syrup is thick. Add lemon juice and remove from heat. Stir in remaining fresh blueberries. Set aside to cool.

Combine powdered sugar and cream cheese. Spread the cream cheese mixture in the bottom of the pie crust. Pour in blueberry mixture and chill. Serve with whipped cream.

Orange cake
This cake has a subtle flavor and light texture.

½ cup of oil
¾ cup of sugar
zest from one orange
2 large eggs
½ cup sour cream
¼ cup orange juice
1 ½ cup flour
1 teaspoon baking powder
½ teaspoon baking soda
½ teaspoon salt

Mix together and bake in a tube pan 350 degrees for 30 minutes.

Madeleines
These tea cakes are said to have inspired Marcel Proust to write Remembrance of Things Past.

8 tablespoons of butter
1 cup of flour
½ teaspoon baking powder
¼ teaspoon salt
3 eggs
2/3 cup sugar
1 tablespoon vanilla

Beat sugar and eggs and then add the rest of the ingredients. Place in shell-shaped Madeleine pans or muffin-top pans. Bake at 375 degrees for 12 minutes. Sprinkle with powdered sugar.

Fruit upside down cake.

Looks great, but very easy to make.

Preheat oven to 350. Grease a round, deep cake pan.
Use apple, pear, peaches, or pineapple.
Cake:

      1 1/3 cup of flour

      2/3 cup sugar

      1 1/2 teaspoon baking powder

      2/3 cup milk

      ½ stick unsalted butter

      1 tablespoon vanilla

Topping:

      Fruit

      2 tablespoon butter

      1/3 cup brown sugar

      1tablespoonp water

Melt sugar and butter in microwave until syrup is formed.
Spread bottom of pan with syrup. Place sliced fruit in
bottom of pan. Cover with cake batter. Bake at 350 for 30
minutes or until done. Cool and turn out cake onto plate.

Indian Pudding   (Slow cooker)

    3 cups of milk
    ½ cup cornmeal
    ½ teaspoon salt
    3 eggs
    ¼ cup brown sugar
    1/3 cup molasses
    ½ teaspoon cinnamon
    2 tabs butter
    ¼ teaspoon allspice
    ½ teaspoon ginger

Boil milk and cornmeal in a saucepan until thickened. Pour in slow cooker and add the rest of ingredients. Cook on slow for 6 to 8 hours.

Visiting Cake

It was common practice at one time when visits to neighbors was a rare occasion to bring along a sweet treat. This recipe was brought to Maine by early Swedish settlers. It makes a flat dense cake.

> 1 cup sugar, plus extra for sprinkling
> Grated zest and juice of 1 lemon
> 2 large eggs
> 1/4 teaspoon salt
> 1 teaspoon soda
> 1 teaspoon pure vanilla extract
> 1 1/4 cup all-purpose flour
> 1 stick (8 tablespoons) unsalted butter, melted and cooled
> About 1/4 cup sliced almonds (blanched or not)

Preheat the oven to 350 degrees. Butter a seasoned a 9-inch cake pan or pie pan. Put the sugar into a medium bowl. Add the zest and juice to sugar and mix on medium speed. Add eggs and then the rest of the ingredients . Place batter in a greased pan. Scatter the sliced almonds over the top and sprinkle with a little sugar Bake the cake for 25 to 30 minutes, or until it is golden and a little crisp on the outside.

Mandarin Orange Cake

This recipe was given to me on a trip to Nova Scotia by church ladies. Easy to make and very tasty.

 1 cup flour
 1 cup sugar
 1 teaspoon baking soda
 1 small can Mandarin oranges with juice
 1 egg
 ½ teaspoon salt

Mix and place in 8x8 greased pan and bake at 350 for 40-50 minutes.

Topping

 2 tablespoons milk
 2 tablespoons butter
 ¾ cup brown sugar

Mix and spread on cake. Put back in oven for 5-10 minutes until topping begins to bubble.

Snickerdoodles
A Christmas Tradition

 2 2/3 cups of flour
 ½ cup softened butter
 ½ cup shortening
 1 ½ cups sugar
 2 eggs
 1 tablespoon vanilla extract
 2 teaspoons cream of tartar
 1 teaspoon baking soda
 ¼ teaspoon salt

Coating: 2 tablespoons white sugar & 2 tablespoons cinnamon

Cream together butter, shortening, sugar with eggs and vanilla. Blend rest of ingredients. Roll dough into balls and roll balls in sugar/cinnamon coating. Place 2 inches apart on cookie sheet. Bake for 8 to 10 minutes.

Coconut Upside-Down Cake

6 tablespoons butter
2/3 cup of brown sugar
2 tablespoons water
1 cup toasted coconut
1 ¼ cups all purpose flour
1 ¼ teaspoon baking powder
½ teaspoon salt
¼ cup butter
1 egg
½ cup milk
1 tablespoon vanilla extract

Spread coconut on baking sheet in a single layer and bake at 325 for five to six minutes until golden brown.

In a saucepan melt 6 tablespoons butter, brown sugar, and water. In an eight inch round cake pan spread the coconut and cover with the brown sugar mixture.

In a mixing bowl, cream butter and sugar, and egg. Add flour, baking powder, and salt and beat for one minute Pour batter over coconut mixture and bake at 350 for 35-40 minutes until done. Cool and turn upside down on plate.

ABOUT THE AUTHOR

Stephen E. Stanley grew up on the Maine coast and graduated from Morse High School in Bath. He attended the University of Southern Maine, Lesley University, the University of New Hampshire, and Columbia Pacific University.

Mr. Stanley was a high school educator for over thirty years and recently retired as the district mentor for secondary education at a large New Hampshire school system.

Also by Stephen E. Stanley

A MIDCOAST MURDER
A Jesse Ashworth Mystery

MURDER IN THE CHOIR ROOM
A Jesse Ashworth Mystery

THE BIG BOYS DETECTIVE AGENCY
A Jesse Ashworth Mystery

JIGSAW ISLAND
A novel of Maine

MURDER ON MT. ROYAL
A Jesse Ashworth Mystery

MURDER AT THE WINDSOR CLUB
A Jeremy Dance Mystery

Made in the USA
Lexington, KY
27 July 2012